FOCUS ON

INSECTS

JANE PARKER

SHOOTING STAR PRESS

INTRODUCTION

Insects have been around for about 370 million years. They thrived in coal forests during the Carboniferous age, and were the first creatures to fly. Through their pollinating activities and also because they spread disease, insects have a major impact on our lives.

Insects number more than all other animals put together, and they are becoming extinct faster than any other group, as the habitats where they live disappear. This book explores the natural history of insects, and provides information about insects related to geography and literature, math and science, history and the arts. The key below shows how these subjects are divided up.

This edition produced in 1996 for
Shooting Star Press Inc
230 Fifth Avenue
Suite 1212
New York, NY 10001

Design	David West Children's Book Design
Designer	Flick Killerby
Series Director	Bibby Whittaker
Editors	Jen Green
Picture Research	Emma Krikler
Illustrator	Dave Burroughs

© Aladdin Books Ltd 1993

Created and produced by
Aladdin Books Ltd
28 Percy Street
London W1P 9FF

First published in the United States in 1993 by Gloucester Press

ISBN 1-57335-539-9

Printed in Belgium

Geography
The symbol of the planet Earth indicates where geographical facts and activities are examined in this book. These sections include a discussion of the vast distances covered by some species of migrating insects.

Language and literature
An open book is the sign for activities and information about language and literature. These sections include a look at the many proverbs and sayings that have been inspired by the characteristics of different species of insects.

Science and technology
The microscope symbol indicates science information or activities. A green symbol shows an environmental issue. These sections give many insights into insect behavior.

History
The sign of the scroll and hourglass indicates historical information. These sections examine how different insects have been helpful and harmful over the ages. Some cultures have even regarded them as sacred.

Math
Activities and information related to mathematics are indicated by the symbol of the ruler, protractor, and compasses. Activities include making a chart based on the life cycles of various species of insects.

Art, craft, and music
The symbol showing a sheet of music and art tools signals where activities and information about art, craft, and music are given. Artists and sculptors have tried to capture the beauty of insects over the centuries, and composers have even written music about them.

CONTENTS

WHAT ARE INSECTS?

Insects are the most successful of all animal groups, making up 85 percent of the whole animal kingdom. There are as many as 10,000 insects living on every square yard of the Earth's surface. There are many different kinds of insects, but all share a common body design, adapted to cope with every possible environment, and to eat every possible kind of food. All adult insects have a segmented body which is divided into three parts: head, thorax, and abdomen.

Antennae (see pages 12-13)

Compound eye (see pages 12-13)

An insect's skin is made of a tough substance called chitin. This forms a hard shell, or exoskeleton, which protects the insect's organs. The leg and wing muscles are securely anchored to the exoskeleton. It is waterproof, and prevents the insect from drying out. But it does not allow air through. Holes in the skin, called spiracles, lead to breathing tubes. The exoskeleton does not grow. As an insect gets bigger, it must shed its old skin, and grow a new one. The outer skin, or cuticle, is patterned and colored for camouflage or warning (see pages 14-15).

Mouthparts (see pages 8-9)

Thorax

Six jointed legs (see pages 10-11)

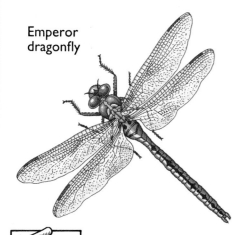

Emperor dragonfly

Common cockroach

Bush cricket

Firebug

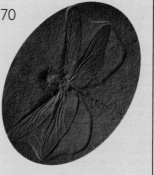

Preserved in stone
Insects first appeared on Earth about 370 million years ago. Early species had no wings; they fed on the sap and spores of the newly-evolved land plants. Insects were the first creatures to conquer the air, 150 million years before birds first flew. This is a fossil of an early dragonfly that lived 300 million years ago, in the steamy Carboniferous forests with the ancestors of the dinosaurs.

All insects have three pairs of jointed legs, and most have four wings. Insects from some easily recognizable insect groups are shown above. The classification of insects is explained on page 30.

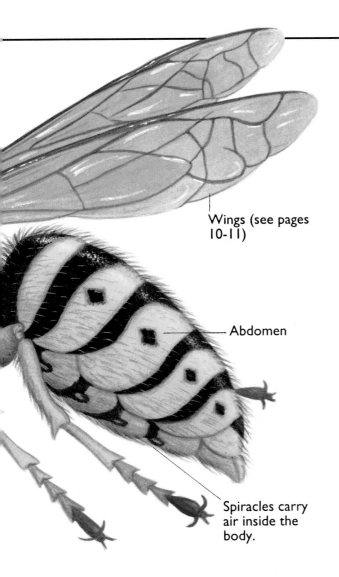

Wings (see pages 10-11)

Abdomen

Spiracles carry air inside the body.

Biblical insects
The Bible contains many stories about Samson, a hero possessed of great strength. One story tells how he killed a young lion that threatened him. Later he noticed bees flying from the lion's body and found honey inside it. He made his discovery into a riddle: 'Out of the eater came forth meat, and out of the strong came forth sweetness.' No one could guess the answer. In fact, the insects were probably not bees at all, but carrion flies that live on rotting flesh. The explanation of the honey is still a mystery!

Samson discovers the bees.

The head contains a simple brain which receives messages from the sense organs and controls the muscles. The thorax is made of three segments fused together. It carries the legs and wings. The abdomen contains the organs for digestion and reproduction.

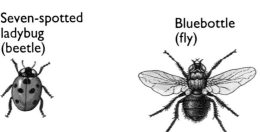

Seven-spotted ladybug (beetle)

Bluebottle (fly)

Privet hawkmoth

Wood ant

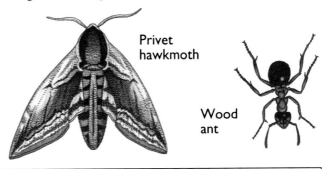

Insect relatives
Insects belong to a group of animals called arthropods. They all have segmented bodies with hard exoskeletons. But the other arthropods pictured here are not insects. Spiders have eight legs. Their body segments are fused in two parts – a head-thorax and an abdomen. Millipedes and centipedes have many body segments, with legs on each.

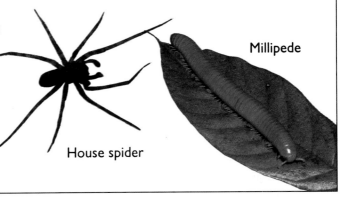

Millipede

House spider

LIFE CYCLES

Insects hatch from eggs. Young insects are eating machines. They consume as much food as they can in order to grow to adulthood as quickly as possible, and shed or molt their skins as they expand. Their goal as adult insects is to mate and lay eggs, and so the life cycle begins again. The change from young to adult form is called metamorphosis. In many species the young insects turn into adults gradually. In some species, however, the change is quite dramatic. These young insects, or larvae, often have a different diet to their parents. They live their early life in a form very different to their adult shape.

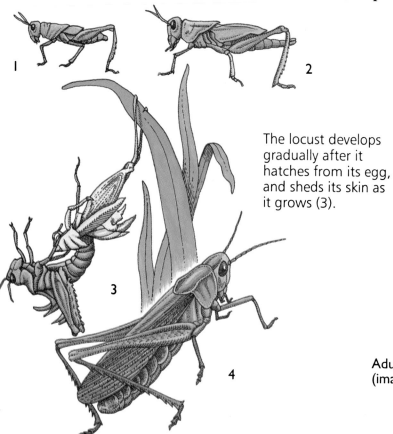

1

2

Egg

The locust develops gradually after it hatches from its egg, and sheds its skin as it grows (3).

3

4

Adult
(imago)

Incomplete metamorphosis

In many species the transformation from young to adult form is gradual. Young locusts are called nymphs. Newly hatched nymphs look a little like small, wingless adults. As they grow, they shed their skin whenever it gets too small. Each time they molt they become more like adults. They emerge from their final molt complete with wings and reproductive organs, ready to fly off, find a mate and lay eggs. This gradual change is incomplete metamorphosis. Cockroaches, bugs, and dragonflies also have incomplete metamorphosis.

Caring parents
Many insect parents go to a lot of trouble to protect their newly-hatched young and provide a ready supply of food. Butterflies lay their eggs on a suitable food plant. Gall wasps choose plants that will grow a protective gall around the larvae. Some wasps paralyze an insect victim and drag it into their burrow for the larvae to feed on. Female cockroaches carry their eggs around with them until they are almost ready to hatch. Earwig mothers carefully clean their eggs and young.

Caterpillar watch (3 months)

Summer is the time to observe the life cycle of butterflies, such as the large white butterfly. You may be lucky enough to find some eggs or caterpillars, and wish to remove them for study and identification. Place them, with the leaves on which you found them, in a box covered with 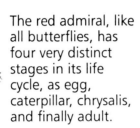 muslin. Keep the box in a cool, moist place and replace the leaves with the same kind every day. Watch the caterpillars grow, and count how many times they molt before they pupate. When the butterflies emerge, watch them unfurl their wings by pumping blood into the veins. Let the butterflies go.

The red admiral, like all butterflies, has four very distinct stages in its life cycle, as egg, caterpillar, chrysalis, and finally adult.

Caterpillar (larva)

Chrysalis (pupa)

Complete metamorphosis

Some kinds of insects undergo a much more dramatic change as they grow, from larvae to adults. As grubs or caterpillars, the young of these species look nothing like adult insects. They eat constantly and molt whenever their skin gets too small. Eventually the larvae anchor themselves to a safe spot by a silken thread, and molt to reveal a chrysalis. The chrysalis looks motionless, but inside a great transformation is going on. Long, jointed legs and antennae form, and wings develop. At last the chrysalis bursts open and a completely different animal emerges. This dramatic change is called complete metamorphosis.

Some species of ichneumon wasps lay their eggs in a living caterpillar. Once hatched, the grubs feed on the caterpillar's insides. The grown larvae burst through the caterpillar's skin, and turn into pupae.

Life charts

The red admiral spends one week as an egg, five weeks as a caterpillar, two weeks as a pupa, and nine months (39 weeks) as an adult. The pie chart below represents this life cycle. Make a similar chart for the stag beetle, which spends two weeks as an egg, three years (156 weeks) as a caterpillar, eight months (35 weeks) as a pupa, and four weeks as an adult. Add the total number of weeks. Work out what percentage each stage is by multiplying each by 100 and dividing by the total of weeks. Then multiply each figure by 3.6 to find out how many degrees it represents of a circle. Mark out the degrees with a protractor.

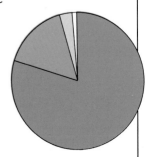

FEEDING

Insects have adapted to make use of every possible food source. Some feed on plants and some on animals. Some suck juices, while some munch on solid food. Many insects consume their prey while it is still alive; many more eat it when it is dead. Some insects are specialized to eat wood or pollen, feathers or blood, even dung. Some eat each other. Many insects feed on humans, causing illness by infecting people with tiny disease organisms. Insects that eat our food can cause famine. Those that eat building materials can cause great damage.

Insect species have different kinds of mouthparts, specialized to cope with their particular diet. All have four main structures. The mandibles are hard jaws for biting, the maxillae are secondary jaws. The labrum and the labium form the upper and lower lips. Caterpillars of butterflies and moths have strong jaws to munch leaves.

Ant

Biting
Ants' saw-shaped mandibles are closed by strong muscles to chomp on solid food. Behind the mandibles, the maxillae taste the food. The labium and labrum chew it and push it into the mouth.

Mandible

Labium

A monarch butterfly caterpillar consumes a leaf.

Food chains
Insects form very important links in food chains, eating plants and in turn being eaten by other insects and larger animals. In temperate climates such as Europe, when the weather warms in spring and the buds on trees begin to burst, thousands of insect eggs hatch into grubs which begin to feed and grow. They provide food for the young of nesting birds such as blackbirds and robins. Swallows return from their warm wintering grounds in South Africa just as the grubs are turning into adult insects. This provides an airborne feast for the swallows (right) to feed to their young as they hatch.

Locust pests

In Africa, the feeding habits of migratory locusts make them one of the most feared of pests. These insects are usually solitary, and dull in color. But when rains come to the parched savannahs and grass begins to grow, they begin to reproduce rapidly, and become brightly colored. They gather in swarms of billions. Such a swarm can strip a field of crops in minutes, leaving the farmer with no food.

Butterfly

Proboscis

Mosquito

Sucking

Butterfly and moth mouthparts have evolved into a long straw-like tube, or proboscis, to enable the insect to suck liquid nectar from flowers. The proboscis is kept rolled up between feeds. The housefly (left) squirts digestive juices down its proboscis onto its food. When the food has gone mushy, the fly sucks it up.

Fly

Piercing

Insects such as shieldbugs and mosquitoes puncture the hard skin of plants or animals to suck out juices. Their mandibles have evolved into needle-like tubes. The insect feels for a suitable place to puncture with the soft labium which surrounds its 'needle.' Then it stabs its prey, and pumps in digestive fluids before it sucks the victim's juices out.

Mandibles

Wood-boring beetles

The furniture beetle lays its eggs in cracks in old, dead wood. The wood provides a food source for the larvae, whether it is a dead tree or a valuable piece of antique furniture. Undetected, the larvae, or 'woodworm,' tunnel through the wood, and eventually pupate. Flight holes suddenly appear in the wood as the adult insects leave to mate and lay eggs on a new food source. Flight holes have sometimes been faked in new furniture, to make it appear older, and therefore more valuable.

Insects as food

Although few people from Western countries consider eating insects, they are nutritious, and are eaten as delicacies in many parts of the world. Australian Aborigines eat adult bogong moths, and the fat 'witchetty' grubs of the giant wood moth. In Africa mosquito pie is eaten, and in Asia stir-fried locust is popular.

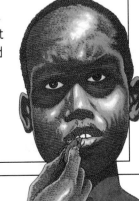

GETTING ABOUT

Insects are masters of land, air, and fresh water. They use their legs and wings to move about efficiently in each environment. Most kinds of insects have two sets of wings for flying, gliding, and hovering. These fragile structures are strengthened by veins. In beetles the front pair of wings has adapted to form hard wing cases. In flies the two hind wings have become balancing organs called halteres. An insect's six legs have strong muscles for walking, running, jumping, and swimming. Some flies can cling upside down because of the hairs and pads on the ends of their legs (see pages 20-21).

Vertical muscles contract, wings flap up.

Horizontal muscles contract, wings flap down.

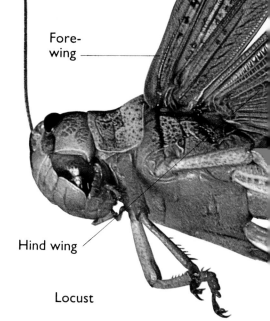

Fore-wing

Hind wing

Locust

Flapping the wings

Horizontal and vertical muscles are attached internally to the hard skeleton of the insect's thorax, which acts like a 'click box.' The sets of muscles contract alternately to make the insect's wings beat powerfully and rapidly. When the vertical muscles contract to pull down the roof of the thorax, it springs inward and the wings are flipped upward. When the horizontal muscles contract, the ends of the thorax are pulled in; the roof 'clicks' back to its domed shape and the wings are flapped downward.

Flight music
The Flight of the Bumble Bee is a piece of music by Rimsky-Korsakov. This Russian composer based his operas on fairy tales and folk-legends, and used the orchestra to make the sounds in the stories. The piece has a fast time, or tempo, which imitates the rapid buzzing of a bee's wings as it flies up and down looking for flowers.

Caterpillar tread
Many caterpillars have three pairs of proper legs at the front of their bodies, and five pairs of false legs, with suckers on the end, at the rear. The caterpillar moves one pair of legs at a time, distributing its weight equally over the other legs. This allows it to move over obstacles in its way. 'Caterpillar tracks' based on the same principle are used on heavy vehicles like bulldozers, tractors, and army tanks. They distribute the vehicle's weight evenly, so it can travel over rough or slippery ground.

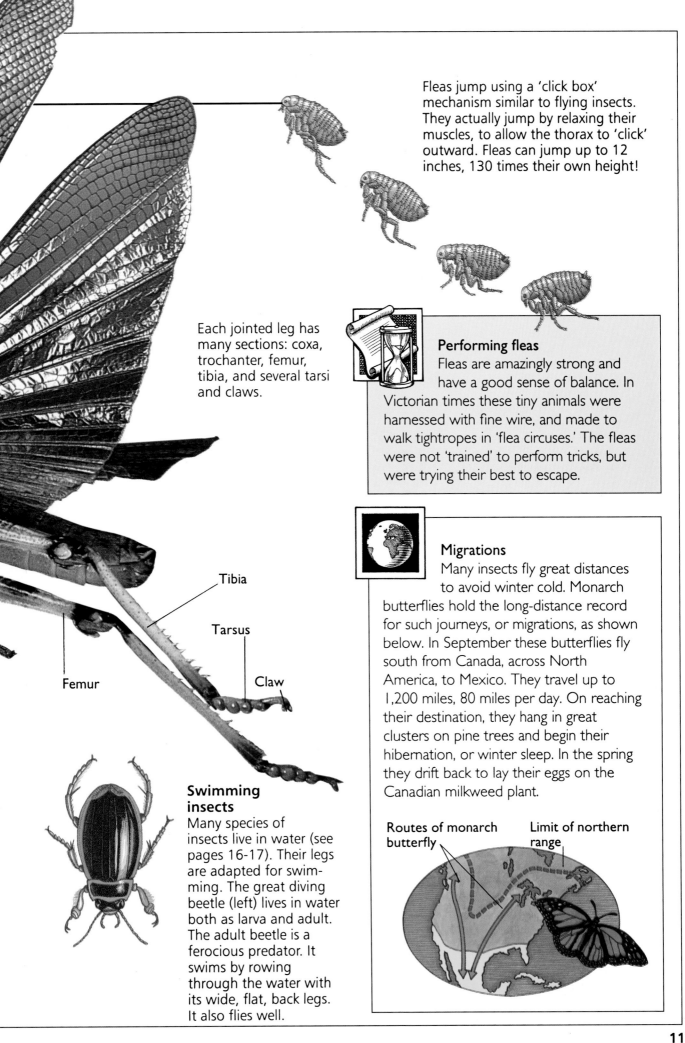

Fleas jump using a 'click box' mechanism similar to flying insects. They actually jump by relaxing their muscles, to allow the thorax to 'click' outward. Fleas can jump up to 12 inches, 130 times their own height!

Each jointed leg has many sections: coxa, trochanter, femur, tibia, and several tarsi and claws.

Performing fleas
Fleas are amazingly strong and have a good sense of balance. In Victorian times these tiny animals were harnessed with fine wire, and made to walk tightropes in 'flea circuses.' The fleas were not 'trained' to perform tricks, but were trying their best to escape.

Tibia

Tarsus

Claw

Femur

Migrations
Many insects fly great distances to avoid winter cold. Monarch butterflies hold the long-distance record for such journeys, or migrations, as shown below. In September these butterflies fly south from Canada, across North America, to Mexico. They travel up to 1,200 miles, 80 miles per day. On reaching their destination, they hang in great clusters on pine trees and begin their hibernation, or winter sleep. In the spring they drift back to lay their eggs on the Canadian milkweed plant.

Swimming insects
Many species of insects live in water (see pages 16-17). Their legs are adapted for swimming. The great diving beetle (left) lives in water both as larva and adult. The adult beetle is a ferocious predator. It swims by rowing through the water with its wide, flat, back legs. It also flies well.

Routes of monarch butterfly

Limit of northern range

SENSES

In order to survive, insects must sense the world around them, through sight, smell, hearing, taste, and touch. They are also sensitive to ultraviolet light, to magnetism and gravity, temperature and humidity. Many insect sense organs are extremely acute. In each species they are tuned to the range of sensations most useful for survival. Messages from sense organs all over an insect's body pass along nerve fibers to the simple brain in its head. Insects cannot 'think.' They carry out predetermined responses to messages received from the sense organs, to feed, mate, lay eggs, attack, or escape.

Sensitive hairs
The heads, bodies, and legs of houseflies, like most insects, are covered by hairs which are sensitive to movements in the air.

Compound eye
There are about 4,000 facets or lenses in a fly's eye. A bee has 5,000, a dragonfly has 30,000. Some ants have only nine.

Antennae

Taste organs are found on the feet.

Halteres
The fly's club-shaped halteres are modified hind wings which vibrate to balance the insect, and measure its speed, and direction of flight.

Most insects have simple eyes which perceive only light and dark shadows. They also have compound eyes, made up of hundreds or thousands of lenses, each seeing a slightly different view of the world. With these two different kinds of eyes, most insects can see all around them, in color, in fine detail, and even in the dark. The other main insect sense organs are the antennae. These projections are often covered with hairs, attached to nerve fibers which send messages to the brain whenever the hair is moved. There are also tiny hairs that are chemically sensitive to smells. The antennae also monitor moisture in the air.

Taste sensors are found on the mouthparts and often on the feet. Some insects have eardrums for hearing sounds. Others have hairs which are so sensitive that they can detect the air movements, or vibrations, made by sounds.

Through animal eyes
Insects see the world differently to other animals, such as birds and cats. Birds see in full color, with detail only in the center of the field of vision. Birds such as hawks can see small prey from a great distance (below). Cats focus well across a central, horizontal strip of their eye's retina. They see only dull colors. Each lens of an insect's compound eye sees the small scene in front of it. The brain merges the images to build up a detailed, three-dimensional picture.

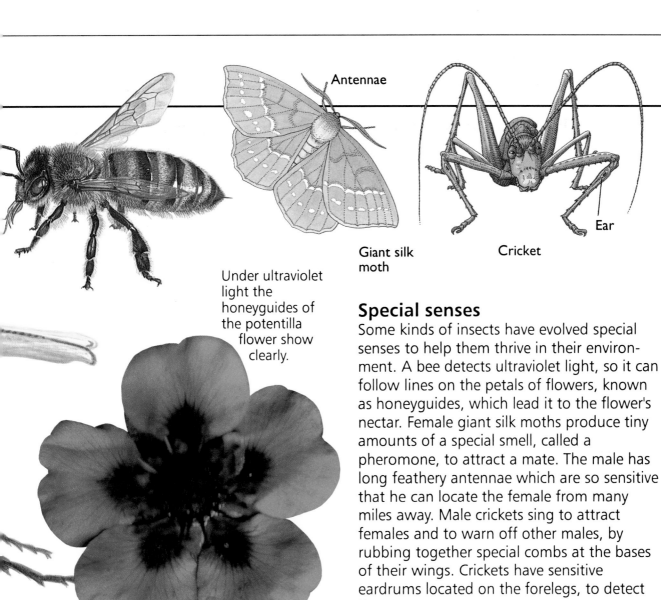

Antennae

Ear

Giant silk moth

Cricket

Under ultraviolet light the honeyguides of the potentilla flower show clearly.

Special senses

Some kinds of insects have evolved special senses to help them thrive in their environment. A bee detects ultraviolet light, so it can follow lines on the petals of flowers, known as honeyguides, which lead it to the flower's nectar. Female giant silk moths produce tiny amounts of a special smell, called a pheromone, to attract a mate. The male has long feathery antennae which are so sensitive that he can locate the female from many miles away. Male crickets sing to attract females and to warn off other males, by rubbing together special combs at the bases of their wings. Crickets have sensitive eardrums located on the forelegs, to detect the song.

Literary crickets

In Victorian times crickets often lived in houses. People thought disaster would befall the family if they stopped their song. Charles Dickens' story *The Cricket in the Hearth* describes a cricket merrily joining in with the kettle singing on the hearth.

Katydid crickets are named after the sound they produce. Two of these crickets 'discussing' whether 'Katy did' or 'Katy didn't' prompted the author Susan M. Coolidge to tell the sorry story of *What Katy Did*. Jiminy Cricket is a character in the Walt Disney film of Pinocchio, about a wooden puppet whose nose grew bigger every time he told a lie. The film is based on a story by Carlo Collodi.

Human vision

Cat vision

Insect vision

Human vision

POISONS AND STINGS

Animals use poisons for two reasons: to defend themselves against predators, and to overcome their own prey. Insects are no exception to this. Some have poisonous stings in their tails, some bite with poisonous jaws. Others are just poisonous all over. Insects that use poisons to catch prey are often masters of disguise. Those that use poisons for defense usually advertise the fact by having bright warning colors on their bodies, usually red- or yellow-and-black. Other insects are not poisonous, but mimic those that are (see page 22).

Hor

Bee stings

Worker honeybees will defend the hive quite literally with their lives. The sting at the end of the worker bee's abdomen is a sac full of poison connected by a tube to a sharp, barbed spine. When the bee stings, the barbs make sure the sting stays in the victim while the venom is pumped into the wound. But they also mean that when the bee flies off, the end of its abdomen is torn away and it then dies.

Plates pump venom

Bulb full of venom

Venom sac

Worker bee

Sting remedies

Bees and wasps only sting when they feel threatened, so you are more likely to get stung if you shout or wave your arms to drive one away. If you are stung by a bee, remove the sting with tweezers, taking care not to squeeze the poison sac. Wasps will not leave their sting in your skin if you allow them to remove it.

Wash the wound thoroughly with antiseptic, and put a cold, damp cloth on it to relieve the pain. Bee and wasp stings are not dangerous unless the swelling blocks the throat, or unless the victim who has been stung has an allergy to insect stings.

Lethal weapon

The bodies of some kinds of insects are poisonous, and taste disgusting. This provides a good defense against predators who recognize the species, and do not attack it. Some squirt stinging liquids, others have irritating hairs that get stuck in an attacker's skin. The grubs of a South African leaf beetle are so poisonous that Kalahari bushmen (right) use them to tip the ends of their arrows.

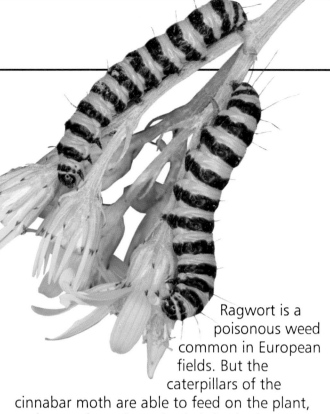

Ragwort is a poisonous weed common in European fields. But the caterpillars of the cinnabar moth are able to feed on the plant, and store the poisons in their body tissues. A bird who eats one will become very sick. These caterpillars have yellow-and-black warning stripes on their bodies to advertise their identity. Birds learn after only one experience to leave them alone.

Insects in folklore medicine

The bodies of blister beetles contain an irritating fluid called cantharidin which these insects use to defend themselves against predators. Before modern medicines were developed, doctors used to apply this substance to their patients' skin as a treatment for warts. The blisters caused by the fluid were also thought to allow the escape of poisons that built up inside the body. Bee stings were thought to cure rheumatism, so bees were allowed to sting the inflamed joints of rheumatic patients.

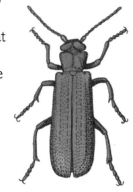

Proverbial insects

Traditional sayings or proverbs often refer to the familiar characteristics of common insects to help describe people's behavior. Groups of people working very hard at a joint task are sometimes called 'busy bees.' If someone has a particular concern which others may not share, they are said to have a 'bee in their bonnet.' Children who will not sit still and concentrate at school are said to have 'ants in their pants.' Can you describe someone who has a 'butterfly mind?'

Bee in your bonnet

Beetle chemists

Bombardier beetles use a spectacular chemical reaction as a powerful weapon against attackers. The beetle has special chambers in its abdomen where it stores two chemicals, each fairly harmless on its own. When the beetle is alarmed it mixes the chemicals in another chamber, together with an enzyme, which aids the reaction. A rocket-like jet of hot, poisonous spray shoots from the end of the abdomen. The beetle can direct the spray by twisting its abdomen towards a victim. The boiling chemicals produced cause painful blisters.

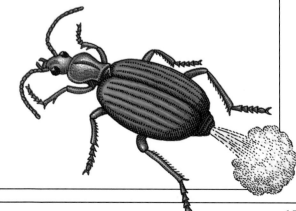

BUGS

Bugs are a particular group of insects that share a common feature: they all pierce their plant or animal food, and suck the juices with mouthparts formed into a beak or long nose, called a rostrum. The front pair of wings in many bugs is divided into two halves, a hard front part and a delicate, transparent back part. This gives the group its scientific name, Hemiptera or half-wing. Cicadas, hoppers, aphids, and scale insects are all members of this family. Bugs undergo incomplete metamorphosis, and the young look very similar to adults. Many bugs are serious pests. Some, such as aphids, devastate plants; others carry disease, such as the assassin bugs of South America.

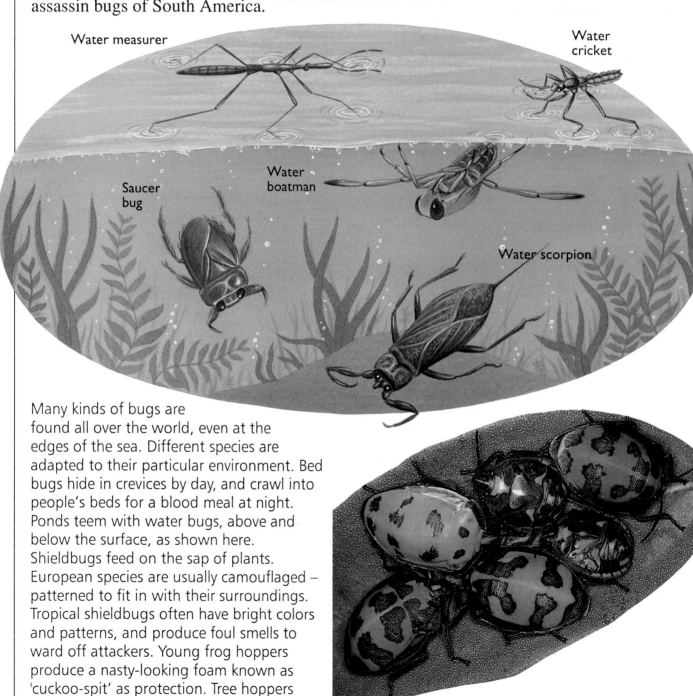

Water measurer

Water cricket

Saucer bug

Water boatman

Water scorpion

Many kinds of bugs are found all over the world, even at the edges of the sea. Different species are adapted to their particular environment. Bed bugs hide in crevices by day, and crawl into people's beds for a blood meal at night. Ponds teem with water bugs, above and below the surface, as shown here. Shieldbugs feed on the sap of plants. European species are usually camouflaged – patterned to fit in with their surroundings. Tropical shieldbugs often have bright colors and patterns, and produce foul smells to ward off attackers. Young frog hoppers produce a nasty-looking foam known as 'cuckoo-spit' as protection. Tree hoppers disguise themselves as thorns.

Many species of bugs live in or on the surface of fresh water. Water crickets and water measurers have water-repellent feet which do not penetrate the surface of the water. They use their feet and antennae to sense the ripples caused by a drowning insect. Once a victim is located, it is stabbed with the insect's piercing mouthparts and its juices are sucked out. Different species of water bugs prey on tadpoles, beetle larvae, and other small creatures at different depths in the water.

Insects that live underwater must still breathe air. The water boatman solves this problem by trapping a layer of air in a bubble around its body.

Virgin birth
In the spring, aphid eggs hatch into wingless females. To save time, these insects do not mate or lay eggs, but give birth to live babies. Producing young without mating is called parthenogenesis. It is quite common in insects. Later winged males and females (right) are born. They fly off to mate and lay eggs for the following year.

Great diving beetles (page 11) store air beneath their wings, which can then be taken into the body through the spiracles (pages 4-5). The water scorpion (above) has a long siphon, like a snorkel, on the end of its tail, which it extends up above the surface of the water to breathe.

Opposite page:
This group of harlequin bugs from Australia consists of three red males, a yellow female and two nymphs.

Song of the cicada
On warm summer evenings in tropical lands, in Mediterranean countries, and North America, the song of the male cicada is heard. The organ producing the sound is a 'click box,' like the wing mechanism (see page 10), located in the insect's abdomen. An area of hard cuticle is pulled in by a muscle and 'clicks' out again. Long streams of clicks are produced at different pitches. They are amplified by air sacs in the abdomen. Cicadas have ears on their abdomens so that they can hear others singing. The males sing to attract a mate. Females respond by seeking out the best singer, other males respond by singing louder.

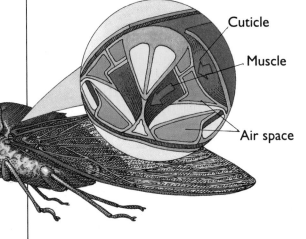

Cuticle

Muscle

Air space

BEETLES

In terms of numbers, the group of beetles, or Coleoptera, has been more successful than any other kind of animal. There are at least 370,000 known species in the world, and new ones are being discovered all the time. Beetles are armor-plated insects. The head and thorax are covered in tough cuticle, formed into strange, threatening shapes in many species. Despite their heavy appearance, most beetles fly very well. Beetle grubs undergo complete metamorphosis to become adult.

Some species of beetles are herbivores (plant-eaters), others are carnivores (meat-eaters). Some kill prey and eat it. Many perform the important function of consuming the dead bodies of animals, some eating the flesh, others eating fur or feathers. Some feed on animal dung. Some beetle pests consume grains or vegetables. Colorado beetles attack potato crops. Others attack vegetation, such as elm bark beetles that spread Dutch elm disease.

Weevil

Burying beetle

Most beetles have biting jaws to seize their prey. In weevils the jaws are located on the end of a long nose or rostrum.

Light show

Glowworms, or fireflies, are neither worms nor flies. They are beetles that produce light to attract mates. During dark evenings, males and females flash signals to each other, like morse code signals from a lantern. The code is different for each species. In Southeast Asia, whole trees pulse with thousands of these tiny lights. The light is made by a chemical reaction involving an enzyme which releases energy in the form of light.

Holy beetle

The female scarab beetle rolls a ball of dung to her burrow. She lays her eggs in the dung, and the larvae feed on it. The scarab beetle was sacred to the ancient Egyptians. They compared the insect's behavior with the action of their god Ra, who, they believed, rolled the sun across the sky each day. Egyptian craftsmen made scarab jewellery, using gold, lapis lazuli, and semiprecious stones.

Rove beetle

Chafer beetle

Many kinds of beetles have fierce-looking jaws and horns. These are often for show, to frighten off predators, or for fighting between males. Stag beetles (left) are so named because the male has fearsome, antlerlike jaws. Sparring stag beetles wrestle, each trying to turn his opponent over. In beetles, the front pair of wings form tough, often colorful wing cases, called elytra. These fold back when the insect is not flying, to protect the delicate wings beneath. In flight, the wing cases are raised.

Insect machines

Some engineers have used insects as inspiration in the design and manufacture of machines. In the late 1940's the vehicle manufacturer Volkswagen pioneered a family car with a rounded beetle shape. Its success was phenomenal, and over 19 million Volkswagen Beetles were produced and exported to nearly 150 countries worldwide.

Elytron

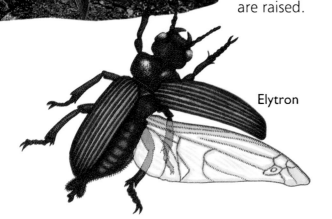

Heralds of death

Deathwatch beetles are wood borers. The larvae live in the dead wood of trees or in cut timber such as the roof timbers of a house. At mating time the males and females call to each other from the tunnels they have bored, tapping their jaws on the wood, and making an ominous ticking noise. In the days before pest control and when illnesses were difficult to treat, this sound in old houses was thought to foretell a death in the family, ticking away the last minutes of someone's life.

FLIES

Flies are not a popular group of insects. Many are not beautiful, some have habits humans find disgusting, and a few carry some of the world's worst diseases. But flies also recycle animal droppings and dead bodies, and pollinate many flowers. True flies, the Diptera, have two small, strong forewings. Their hind wings have become balancing organs, or halteres. Flies are a very versatile group, living almost everywhere in the world, even in the icy wastes of the Arctic.

Flies and disease

Blood-sucking flies transmit some of the world's worst tropical diseases. When they bite an infected person they suck up tiny, disease-causing organisms, which they inject into another person at their next meal, and so the disease is passed on. Tsetse flies transmit sleeping sickness. Their victims experience tiredness and ultimately death. Assassin bugs carry Chagas disease in South America. Malaria, one of the world's most serious diseases, is spread by mosquitoes. Sandflies spread oriental sore or kala-azar, which destroys the skin and internal organs.

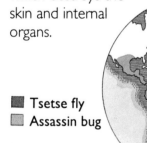

- ■ Tsetse fly
- ▢ Assassin bug

- ■ Malaria mosquito
- ▨ Sandfly

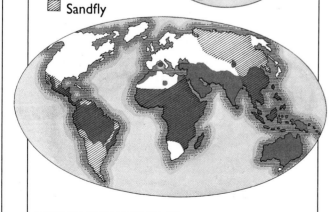

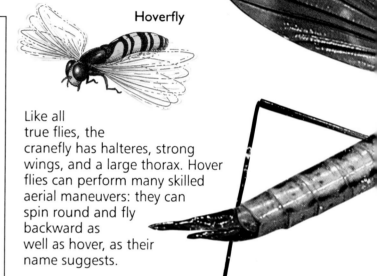

Hoverfly

Like all true flies, the cranefly has halteres, strong wings, and a large thorax. Hover flies can perform many skilled aerial maneuvers: they can spin round and fly backward as well as hover, as their name suggests.

Cranefly

Flies are scavengers, feeding on almost everything: nectar, rubbish, blood, and flesh, dead or alive. They have a sucking proboscis, sometimes converted for piercing their prey. Fly grubs, often called maggots (top left), live in moist places like stagnant mud or rotting meat. They undergo complete metamorphosis to reach their adult state.

Flies are perfectly adapted for flying. They have large eyes and brain for extra control. Their halteres monitor speed, direction, and roll. The wings have special joints which automatically twist the wing blades as they beat, to provide more lift. The enlarged thorax is packed with special flight muscles that contract rhythmically.

Walking on the ceiling

Houseflies and bluebottles have special sticky suction pads and hooks on the ends of their feet so they can crawl up windows or upside down across the ceiling. The hairs all over their body are so sensitive to air movements that they can feel danger, such as a flyswatter, coming just in time to get away.

Hook

Suction pad

Hygiene

It is important to keep food covered if flies are around. House flies feed on rubbish and dung. Their feet and mouthparts become contaminated with germs, that can be transferred onto food and kitchen surfaces if they alight there.

This is a fossil of a long-legged fly once trapped in pine tree resin. The resin has now hardened into amber.

Metamorphosis

The theme of changing from one form to another has intrigued writers and artists for many centuries. The Roman poet, Ovid, wrote a long poem called *Metamorphoses*, 2000 years ago. Based on mythical tales, it tells of characters such as Daphne, who changed into a laurel tree to avoid the attentions of the god Apollo, and Narcissus, who changed into a flower. Artists such as the Spanish painter Salvador Dalí have been inspired by the same theme.

The idea of humans changing into insects has also held horror and fascination. Czech writer Franz Kafka wrote a strange story about a man who wakes up one morning having mysteriously changed into a huge insect overnight. The film called *The Fly* is a horror story about a scientist who slowly becomes a fly.

Fly-eating plants

The Venus flytrap plant lives in the swamps of North America, where the soil is poor. The plant catches flies to supplement its diet with extra nutrients. The flytrap's leaves have sticky, sensitive hairs and toothed edges. When an insect settles to feed, it disturbs the hairs. This triggers the two halves of the leaf to snap together, trapping the insect.

The flytrap's leaves give off a liquid containing digestive chemicals called enzymes, and the insect's body is slowly dissolved and absorbed.

BUTTERFLIES AND MOTHS

Butterflies and moths are called Lepidoptera, which means scale-wings. Their wings are covered with tiny scales, arranged like roof shingles. Some scales have beautiful colors, and others bend light, like crystals, to give a rainbow sheen. Butterflies are generally more colorful than moths. They fly in the daytime, and hold their wings together upright when resting. Their antennae are club-shaped. Moths are active at night. They hold their dull-colored wings flat over their backs when resting. Some male moths have feathery antennae. Butterflies and moths undergo complete metamorphosis.

Owl butterfly
(*Caligo oileus*)

Butterfly mimics

The colorful markings on some butterflies' wings are warning colors, to deter predators. Poisonous insects advertise their distastefulness in this way. Birds soon learn to recognize these species and avoid them. Different species of poisonous moths or butterflies from the same region reinforce the message, by having very similar patterns and wing shapes. In Peru, two poisonous species, of heliconius and podotricha butterflies, look alike. This is called Mullerian mimicry (imitation). Some other butterflies which are not poisonous 'cheat' by mimicking the warning patterns of poisonous species. In North America, a species of harmless viceroy butterfly looks very like the poisonous monarch butterfly. This is called Batesian mimicry.

Podotricha telesiphe

Heliconius telesiphe

Siderone galanthis

Viceroy

Monarch

Butterflies and moths, like all insects, are cold-blooded. Their body temperature is about as warm or cold as their surroundings, since they cannot generate their own body heat, as warm-blooded mammals and birds can. Butterflies spread their wings in the sunshine to warm up and hide in the shade when they are too hot. Moths have furry bodies to retain the heat they absorb during the day, so that they can fly at night.

Disgusting disguises

The young of many moths and butterflies camouflage or disguise themselves as inedible objects, to avoid being eaten by predators. Geometer moth caterpillars look like twigs, and position themselves on branches so as to complete their disguise. The European black hairstreak chrysalis and the hawkmoth caterpillar from Central America (right) pretend to be unpleasant bird droppings.

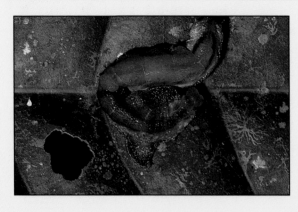

Large elephant hawkmoth

Morpho butterfly (*Morpho menelaus*)

Dasyopthalma rusina

Adapting to industry

The peppered moth is an example of how, over many generations, some species of insects are able to adapt their camouflage to fit in with a changing environment. The normal form of the peppered moth is creamy with dark speckles, difficult to see on the bark of trees. But following the Industrial Revolution in the 19th century, a new form of dark moth became common, which could hide on sooty bark.

Insect painter

Jean Henri Fabré (1823-1915) lived in Provence in France. He was a village school teacher before he turned to entomology, the study of insects. But he did not collect dead insects, like many naturalists of the time. He studied their habits by watching them in the wild.

Fabré wrote many books on insect behavior, describing each detail of their lives. He also left behind many beautiful watercolor paintings of the species he had studied.

Madame Butterfly

The opera *Madame Butterfly* was written by an Italian composer, Giacomo Puccini, in 1904. It tells of a tragic love affair between an American naval officer, Pinkerton, and a Japanese girl, Butterfly. They marry, but Pinkerton leaves, and returns years later with a new wife. Puccini's beautiful melodies convey the drama, passion and tragedy of the story.

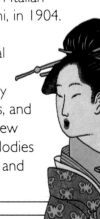

BEES AND WASPS

Bees, wasps, and ants all belong to the same group of insects, called Hymenoptera, meaning transparent wing. Bees and wasps have two pairs of wings, and a narrow 'waist.' Some have yellow-and-black warning colors, and a poisonous sting. The life cycle involves complete metamorphosis. Many species are solitary; honeybees, bumblebees, and common wasps create colonies where the eggs and grubs are cared for by family members.

All bees and some wasps make nests for the young. The sand digger wasp digs holes for its eggs, and the mason bee tunnels in cement. The leaf-cutter bee constructs leaf-lined chambers. Honeybees live in nests, either in holes in trees or in man-made hives. The queen mates with the male drones in flight, and lays her eggs, most of which develop into sterile female workers. Worker honeybees make and repair the nest, and go out to collect pollen and nectar to make into honey, to feed new grubs, and sustain the bees in winter.

Construction work
Honeybees mold perfect hexagonal cells from beeswax, which comes from a gland below their abdomen.

Paper wasps fashion their delicate nests from chewed wood fibers, below.

Wasp

Dancing bees
When a scouting honeybee returns to the hive laden with pollen and nectar, the other worker bees gather to find out the location of the new food. The bee performs a round dance on the vertical surface of the honeycomb. This dance becomes a figure of eight, the bee waggling its rear excitedly as it passes across the center of the figure. The angle of the waggle to the vertical is the same as the angle between the sun, the hive, and the food. The amount of waggling indicates how distant the food source is.

Round dance

The scout stops during the round dance to give the other bees samples of pollen and nectar.

Figure of eight

The queen spends her days laying eggs in comb cells. Her attendant workers feed and clean her.

Spoonful of honey
Before sugar cane was brought to Europe around 700 AD, people used honey to sweeten their food. Egyptian tomb paintings show honey and beeswax being harvested from man-made hives.

Pollination
For a flower's seeds to develop, it must be fertilized by pollen from the same or another flower. The pollen can be dispersed by the wind, or transferred on the bodies of insects such as bees. The insects are attracted by the colors, perfume, and sweet nectar of flowers. As they wander over the petals, their hairy bodies become dusted with powdery pollen. When they visit another flower, the pollen dusts off and pollinates it. The pollinating activities of bees are even more important to the farmer than their honey-making duties.

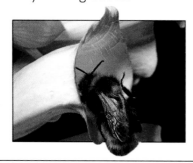

Waspish fashion
Dresses with elegant 'wasp' waists were created in the 19th century by French fashion designer Charles Frederick Worth. The wasp waist was created by a tight corset. Unfortunately, the fashion was extremely uncomfortable, making some women faint.

Pollen baskets
Honeybees have hair and notches on their legs. They use them to comb flower pollen from their heads and bodies, and pack it into pollen baskets, fringed with long, stiff hairs, on each back leg.

ANTS AND TERMITES

Ants belong to the group of Hymenoptera, like bees and wasps. Termites belong to the order of Isoptera, meaning equal wing. Nevertheless, ants and termites have very similar life-styles. They are mainly social insects, living in huge families or colonies, where each insect has a particular job to do. Most do not reproduce; their lives are devoted to caring for their sisters and brothers. Only the queen mates and lays eggs. Her many young, the workers, build, repair, and defend the nest.

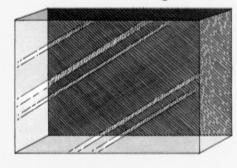

Caste of thousands
Different kinds, or castes, of ants or termites perform different jobs in a colony. Worker ants tend the queen (left), the grubs, and pupae (right). Others clean the nest (above right) and go out in search of food. Soldiers defend the colony.

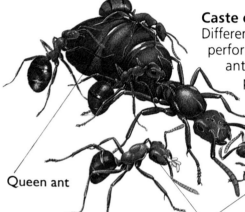

Queen ant

Workers

Pupae

Social ants

Most ants have poor eyesight, but a good sense of smell. They communicate with nest members through touch and through scents called pheromones which they produce. When foraging ants find food, they lay a scent trail for others to follow. Worker ants produce a different scent if they find a damaged part of the nest, which brings others to help with the repair. Ants from one colony recognize each other by their smell, and will attack an intruder from a different colony. They defend themselves by biting and squirting stinging formic acid into the wound they have made. Ants feed on many different types of food. A column of army ants will tear apart and carry off any small creature in its path. Each ant can lift a load many times its own weight.

Making an ant home
You can study ants more easily by building an ant home from a glass tank or plastic box. Cover the outside of the tank with dark paper. Half-fill the tank with earth, and stock it with small black or red ants from the garden. Add damp soil and leaves. After a few days, remove the paper, to see the tunnels built against the sides.

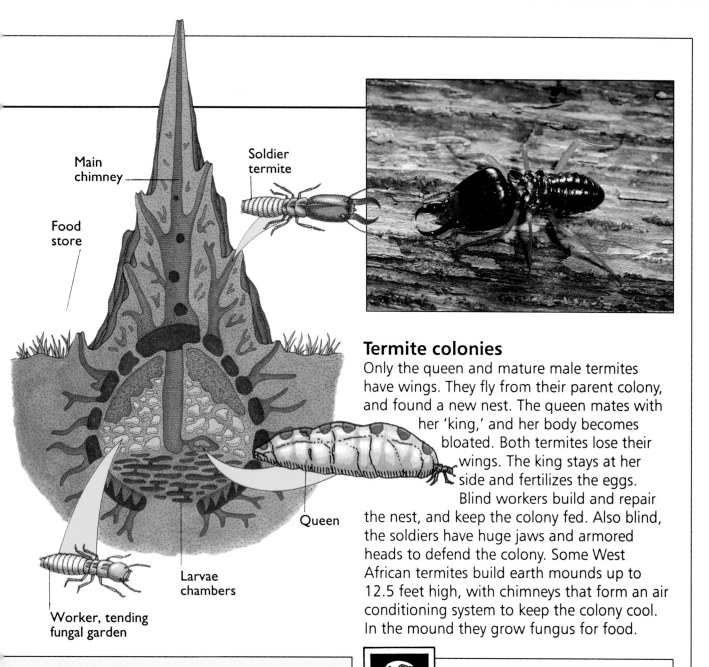

Main
chimney

Food
store

Soldier
termite

Worker, tending
fungal garden

Larvae
chambers

Queen

Termite colonies

Only the queen and mature male termites have wings. They fly from their parent colony, and found a new nest. The queen mates with her 'king,' and her body becomes bloated. Both termites lose their wings. The king stays at her side and fertilizes the eggs.

Blind workers build and repair the nest, and keep the colony fed. Also blind, the soldiers have huge jaws and armored heads to defend the colony. Some West African termites build earth mounds up to 12.5 feet high, with chimneys that form an air conditioning system to keep the colony cool. In the mound they grow fungus for food.

Feed ants on ripe fruit, meat, or jam, and provide fresh leaves and water on damp kitchen paper. Keep your tank in a cool place, and cover it when you are not studying ant behavior, so air can get in, but the ants can't escape. If you have managed to catch a large queen with your stock, the colony should go on indefinitely, and may even produce a swarm of winged ants in the summer. Let them go to produce a new nest.

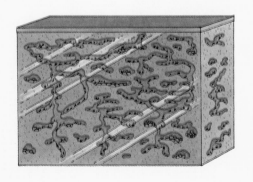

Anteaters of the world

Ants and termites are food for any animal with strong claws to rip open the nests, and a long, sticky tongue to lick the insects out. In Central and South America, armadillos and giant anteaters (below) live on the savannah, and collared anteaters are found in the forests. The aardvark lives off the same diet in South Africa, and the pangolin in Asia. The spiny anteater lives in Australia.

INSECTS AND PEOPLE

Humans have lived with insects since we first evolved. Our ancestors must have battled against biting fleas and scavenging cockroaches, just as we do today. Many insects are pests; some spread disease, some damage property, others consume crops. But insects also play a very positive role. They provide a vital food source for animals such as birds and reptiles. Some pollinate flowers, some dispose of waste matter. Insects provide silk and honey, and delight our eyes and ears. The world would not be the same without them. But as the world's wild places are disappearing, so are many insect species.

We call insects pests when they become so numerous that they begin to threaten human health and comfort. There are thousands of insect pests. They range from the irritating houseflies and head lice which can infest our homes and bodies, causing discomfort, to mosquitoes and locusts which cause death and widespread devastation. Many insects only become pests because humans choose to cultivate the food they eat on a large scale, providing hundreds of acres, or tons, of their usual diet.

Head louse

Egg

Agricultural pests

There are many serious insect crop pests around the world. Some eat the leaves or roots of plants. Others infect the plant with virus disease. Both result in crop failure, with financial losses in richer nations and starvation in developing countries. Rice and maize (sweetcorn) are two of the most important crops in the world. The brown plant hopper damages rice harvests, while the corn leaf hopper is a serious pest of maize crops. The Colorado beetle devastated North American potato crops in the 19th century, until the use of pesticides finally brought it under control.

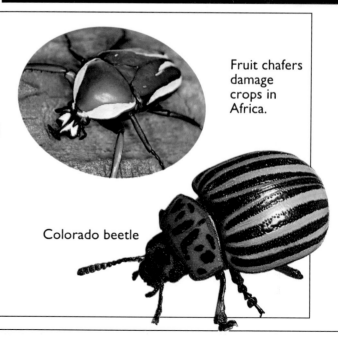

Fruit chafers damage crops in Africa.

Colorado beetle

The silk moth lays her eggs on the leaves of mulberry trees. When the caterpillars hatch they feed on the leaves.

Dependable insects

Some insects have proved very useful to humans, both in the past and today. Without honeybees we would have no honey or beeswax (see pages 24-25). The red food dye cochineal is made from the crushed bodies of a species of scale insects that live on South American cactus plants. It was used by the Aztecs 600 years ago. Modern scientists breed a tiny fruit fly, called drosophila, to help them understand genetic, or inherited, diseases in humans.

Cochineal insects

Like some other insect larvae, the caterpillar of the silk moth produces silk, wrapping itself in a silken cocoon when it is ready to pupate. The Chinese began farming silkworm for this fiber 5,000 years ago. The silk from a silkworm cocoon is 0.001in thick and over 3,000ft long. It is unwound from the cocoon, treated, and woven into a fine fabric. Silk looks and feels beautiful. It is also the strongest of all natural fibers, being warm in cold weather, cool in warm weather, and resistant to burning.

Pest control

For centuries people have used noxious substances to kill insects. Advances in chemistry this century led to the production of chemicals such as DDT, that devastated pests, but also affected other animals. Today chemists produce specialized insecticides which only affect the pests they target. There is also renewed interest in controlling pests through the introduction of other insects that prey on them. Ladybugs can be used to reduce rose aphid populations (below), and tiny parasitic wasps to control greenhouse white flies.

The Black Death

The Bubonic Plague is a fatal disease caused by bacteria. It is transmitted to humans by fleas which have fed on the blood of infected rats. In the sixth century this disease spread across Europe and Asia, killing 100 million people. Another outbreak in the 14th century, known as the Black Death, killed almost half the population of Europe.

CLASSIFICATION OF INSECTS

Scientists classify insects into groups that share similar characteristics, such as appearance and behavior. All insects belong to the animal kingdom under the class *Insecta*. This class is divided into 31 orders, which appear below. The names of the orders are indicated in bold type. The orders are subdivided into genera, and the genera into closely related species, or individual kinds of insects. The chart below shows a typical insect from each order, identified in normal type.

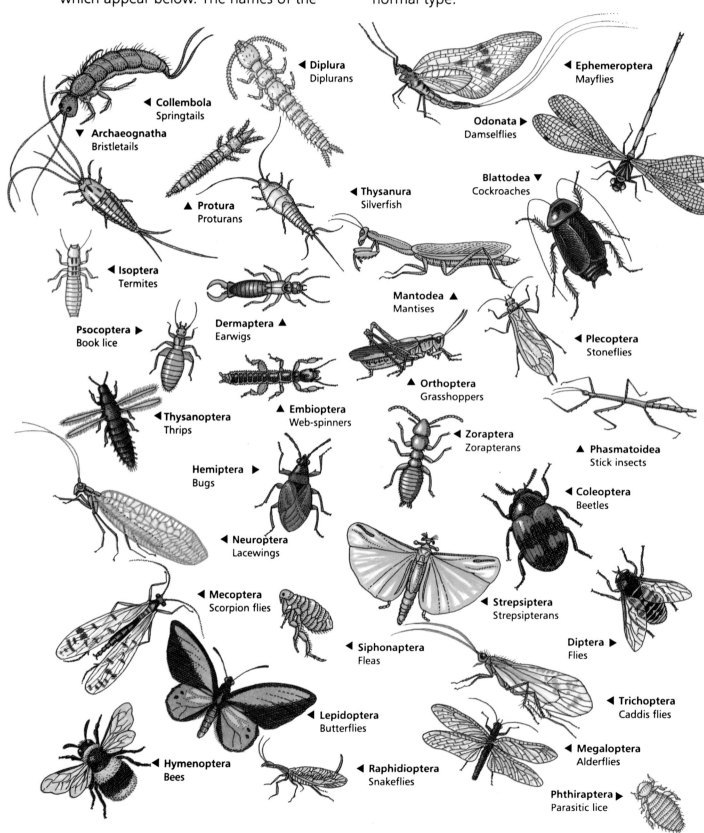

◄ **Diplura**
Diplurans

◄ **Collembola**
Springtails

▼ **Archaeognatha**
Bristletails

▲ **Protura**
Proturans

◄ **Thysanura**
Silverfish

◄ **Ephemeroptera**
Mayflies

Odonata ►
Damselflies

Blattodea ▼
Cockroaches

◄ **Isoptera**
Termites

Mantodea ▲
Mantises

Psocoptera ►
Book lice

Dermaptera ▲
Earwigs

◄ **Plecoptera**
Stoneflies

◄ **Thysanoptera**
Thrips

▲ **Embioptera**
Web-spinners

▲ **Orthoptera**
Grasshoppers

◄ **Zoraptera**
Zorapterans

▲ **Phasmatoidea**
Stick insects

Hemiptera ►
Bugs

◄ **Coleoptera**
Beetles

◄ **Neuroptera**
Lacewings

◄ **Mecoptera**
Scorpion flies

◄ **Strepsiptera**
Strepsipterans

Diptera ►
Flies

◄ **Siphonaptera**
Fleas

◄ **Trichoptera**
Caddis flies

◄ **Lepidoptera**
Butterflies

◄ **Megaloptera**
Alderflies

◄ **Hymenoptera**
Bees

◄ **Raphidioptera**
Snakeflies

Phthiraptera ►
Parasitic lice

GLOSSARY

Abdomen The rear part of an insect's body which contains the internal organs for digestion, excretion, and reproduction.

Camouflage Patterns, colors, and shapes on an insect's body that make it blend in with the background, so it is difficult to see.

Carnivore An animal that eats only other animals.

Elytra The hard pair of wing-cases that cover a beetle's wings.

Entomology The study of insects.

Enzymes Special chemicals made by living things that help chemical reactions to take place.

Exoskeleton The hard outside skin of the bodies of insects and their relatives that protects and supports their soft parts.

Gall A swelling made by some plants when attacked by insects such as tiny wasps.

Herbivore An animal that eats only plants.

Labium The part that forms the top of an insect's mouth, or upper 'lip.'

Labrum The part that forms the bottom of an insect's mouth, or lower 'lip'.

Larvae The young grubs, maggots, or caterpillars of insects that undergo complete metamorphosis.

Mandibles A pair of jaws that bite together in front of an insect's mouth.

Maxilla A second pair of jaws, behind the mandibles, in front of an insect's mouth.

Metamorphosis The transformation of a young insect to an adult.

Migration A journey undertaken by an animal to avoid bad conditions such as extreme cold or heat, or lack of food or water.

Nymph The young of insects that undergo incomplete metamorphosis.

Parasite A plant or animal which eats another plant or animal while it is still alive.

Pheromones Special scents given off by animals at certain times, such as in the breeding season, to communicate with others.

Polarized light Light waves that vibrate in the same plane. Humans cannot tell it from unpolarized light that vibrates in all planes, but many insects can.

Predator An animal that kills and eats other animals for food.

Prey An animal hunted for food.

Proboscis A tube formed from the mouthparts of insects such as flies and butterflies, used to suck up liquid food.

Pupa The chrysalis stage, between the larva and the adult, in insects that undergo complete metamorphosis.

Rostrum The rigid, needlelike tube formed from the mouthparts of insects such as bugs, used to pierce and suck up juices.

Spiracles Holes in the exoskeleton which lead to breathing tubes within an insect's body.

Thorax The middle part of an insect's body, to which the wings and legs are attached.

Trachea Breathing tubes that branch inside an insect's body, carrying air to the muscles and organs.

INDEX

Photocredits
The majority of the pictures are from Bruce Coleman Ltd apart from pages: Front cover bottom, 25 top, 29 top left: Roger Vlitos; 3 middle, 19 top: Robert Harding Picture Library; 5 top: Hulton Deutsch; 8 top, 13 top: Science Photo Library; 9 left, 25 bottom, 28 bottom left: Planet Earth Pictures; 10 bottom: H. Leverton Ltd; 14, 19 bottom: Frank Spooner Pictures; 17 bottom, 29 top right: Oxford Scientific Films; 18 top: Spectrum Colour Library.